MUMMIES
ALL WRAPPED UP

CONTENTS

By Lanny Boutin

MUMMIES
ALL WRAPPED UP

Many ancient cultures believed in an afterlife: another world where people go after they die. Some also believed that people must take their body undamaged with them. But nature has other ideas.

When a person or animal dies, the body's own bacteria begin to consume it. Eventually only the skeleton is left behind. So, to assist in the trip to the afterlife, people started preserving, or mummifying, their dead.

Mummies have been found all over the world. Some were naturally mummified. Others went through elaborate, lengthy ceremonies on their way to becoming mummies.

But, no matter how they were created, mummies hold the answers to a lot of important questions about the past, such as what people looked like and how they lived their lives.

a 3000-year-old mummy from China

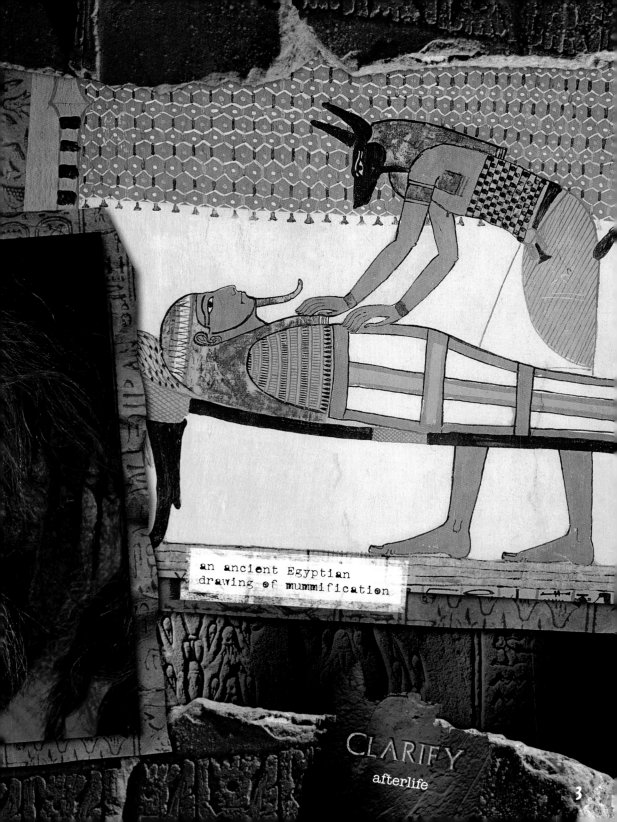

an ancient Egyptian
drawing of mummification

CLARIFY

afterlife

3

EGYPTIAN MUMMIES

Predict:

What do you think this chapter will tell you about Egyptian mummies?

Discovering Tutankhamun

The mummy of Tutankhamun was discovered in 1922 in the Valley of the Kings in Egypt. Workers uncovered a lone stair. Believing it must lead somewhere, they dug down through layers of sand and rubble to reach a sealed door. The name "Nebkheprure" was written on the door's seals. This was the name taken by Tutankhamun, better known as King Tut. King Tut was a pharaoh of Egypt more than three thousand years ago.

The leader of the dig, Howard Carter, hoped they had found King Tut's tomb. Lord Carnarvon, a wealthy collector who had paid for the dig, watched on hopefully.

The workers pried open the door. Behind it they found a small corridor leading to a second door. Its seals had been broken. It looked as if it had been opened by someone, possibly tomb raiders, and then resealed, maybe more than once.

Using only a candle for light, Carter peered through a small hole he had cut in the door. The tomb was dark, but even in the dim light he could see that it held many wonderful treasures.

CLARIFY

pharaoh

OPINION

Do you think Carter should have cut a hole in the door of the tomb? Why or why not?

TUTANKHAMUN'S TOMB

burial chamber

annexe

treasury

antechamber

corridor

hidden steps

Tutankhamun's mummy was found in the burial chamber. The other rooms of the tomb were filled with treasures.

5

The mummy of King Tut was not the first to be found in Egypt. Archaeologists had unearthed many others before. But unlike the others, whose graves had been robbed of everything of value, Tut's burial tomb was almost untouched.

The young king was only nine years old when he was crowned, and just seventeen or eighteen when he died. His tomb contained about 3000 objects, including chairs, stools, boxes, stone vases and baskets. Buried with him were 413 little figurines, called *shabtis*. The Egyptians believed these shabtis would do Tut's chores in the afterlife. There was one shabti for every day of the year, plus extras to oversee them.

The tomb also contained a shrine guarded by the Egyptian god Anubis and many model boats and maps of the underworld to help Tut in his journey.

first shrine

second shrine

fourth shrine

a model boat from the tomb

INFERENCE

. . . unlike the others . . . Tut's burial tomb was almost untouched . . .

What can you infer about Tut's tomb?

Tut's death mask

—— third shrine

—— lid of sarcophagus

top of first coffin

top of second coffin

top of third coffin

mummy and mask

bottom of third coffin

bottom of second coffin

bottom of first coffin

rcophagus ———

Tut's sarcophagus had been laid inside four shrines. Inside his sarcophagus were three hand-carved, wooden coffins, one inside the other. These were inlaid with gold and precious stones. The inner coffin was made almost entirely of gold. Wrapped inside Tut's bandages were 143 gold amulets and other pieces of jewellery. He wore a traditional death mask made of solid gold with blue glass inlaid in the headdress and beard. It weighed 10 kilograms.

Carter and his men carefully catalogued and removed each artefact from the tomb. This process took ten years.

CLARIFY

sarcophagus

How Egyptian Mummies Were Made

When a person or animal dies, moisture and bacteria cause the body to break down. Only the skeleton is left behind. Ancient Egyptians believed that the dead lived on in the next world. Their *ka*, or soul, travelled through this world and was reborn again at dawn, just like the sun each morning. They also believed that the person's ka would find its body in the afterlife, but the ka had to be able to recognise the body. This made its careful preservation very important.

It took the Egyptians 70 days to make a mummy. First the body was brought to a special tent called an *ibu*, where it was washed. The lungs, liver, stomach and intestines were removed through a cut in the abdomen. They were washed, wrapped in bandages and put into Canopic jars. The jars were filled with natron, a natural salt similar to baking soda. The natron dried and preserved the body parts.

CLARIFY

Canopic jars

QUESTION

How do you know the Egyptians took great care in making mummies?

Canopic jars

The heart, which the Egyptians believed was responsible for thinking and feeling, was left in the body. The brain, which they thought was useless, was removed through the nose with a long hook, and thrown away. The inside of the body was then packed with rags or sawdust and buried in natron for 40 days, to dry it out.

When the body was completely dry, scented oils were rubbed into the skin to soften it and make it smell better. The body was then wrapped in cloth bandages. Amulets were carefully tucked between the layers of cloth. These amulets were often images of Egyptian gods. The bandages were then covered with a thick, sticky resin. This process was repeated up to six times.

To make the wrapped body recognisable to the ka, a plaster death mask was painted to look like the person and placed on the head.

CLARIFY
amulets

INFERENCE
What can you infer about the people who prepared the mummies?

HOW EGYPTIAN MUMMIES WERE MADE

1.

Purification: the body was washed in an ibu with natron solution, while priests chanted.

2.

Removal of Organs: stomach, intestines, lungs and liver were removed through a cut in the abdomen then put into Canopic jars with natron.

3.

Removal of the Brain: the brain was removed with a hook through the nose.

4.

Drying: the body was packed with rags or sawdust and buried in natron for 40 days.

5.

Anointing: the skin was massaged with perfumed oils. The mummy could then be covered with jewellery.

6.

Bandaging: the body was wrapped with bandages and amulets were tucked between the layers.

7.

Death Mask: a death mask painted to look like the person was placed on the head.

8.

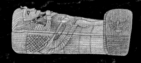

Coffin: the mummy was put in painted wooden coffins and placed in a sarcophagus.

VISUAL CHALLENGE
What other ways could you show this information?

OTHER TYPES OF MUMMIES

Predict

What other types of mummies do you think you will find out about in this chapter?

Cat Mummies

The Egyptians didn't only mummify people. They also mummified cats. The Egyptians considered cats sacred. They protected their food from mice and rats. The Egyptians also believed that cats protected the world from darkness and evil. When the sun set each night, they believed a cat helped the sun god defeat the serpent of darkness so the sun could rise again.

The dead cat was wrapped in strips of cloth. Sometimes the strips were dyed different colours and woven, creating beautiful patterns. Palm leaves were often used to represent ears. The cat's head was then covered with a plaster mask so its ka could find it again.

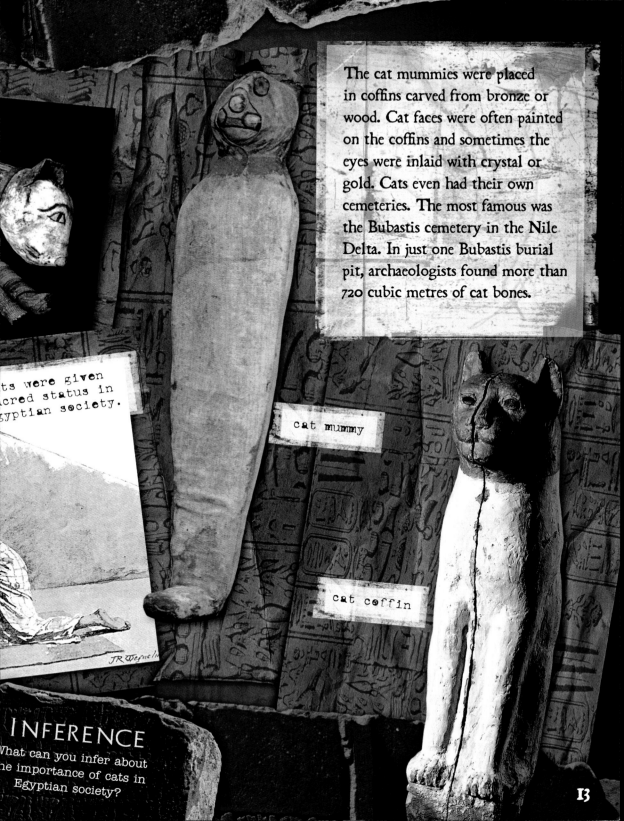

The cat mummies were placed in coffins carved from bronze or wood. Cat faces were often painted on the coffins and sometimes the eyes were inlaid with crystal or gold. Cats even had their own cemeteries. The most famous was the Bubastis cemetery in the Nile Delta. In just one Bubastis burial pit, archaeologists found more than 720 cubic metres of cat bones.

...ts were given
...cred status in
...gyptian society.

cat mummy

cat coffin

INFERENCE

What can you infer about the importance of cats in Egyptian society?

Mummies from Other Cultures

Egyptians were not the first people to make mummies. The Chinchorros were a fishing tribe who lived along the Pacific Coast near Peru and Chile. They started mummifying their relatives as early as 5000 BC. That's 7000 years ago.

They would take each body apart, removing the flesh and setting aside the skin. The body parts were then dried in the sun. When the parts were completely dry, they would reassemble the bones. They would then stretch the skin, stuffed with vegetable matter, over them. Each mummy got a wig and its body was covered with a white ash paste. The skin was then painted with manganese to make it look black. About 2500 BC, the Chinchorros started using red ochre to make red mummies instead of black.

Both adults and children were mummified in Chinchorro culture.

QUESTION
Why do you think the Chinchorro mummies were given a wig?

How Chinchorro Mummies Were Made

Black Mummies

Red Mummies

The head, arms, legs and skin were removed.

Incisions were made in the body and the organs were removed.

The skull was cut open, and the brain was removed.

The head was cut from the body and the brain was removed.

The body was dried in the sun.

The body was reassembled and stuffed with materials such as clay and feathers.

The body was packed with sticks and other materials and the incisions were sewn up.

A wig was placed on the mummy's head.

The body was covered with a white ash paste.

The head was reattached to the body.

The mummy was painted black.

The mummy was painted red.

Visual Challenge
What other ways could you show this information?

15

Across the Atlantic Ocean, on the Canary Islands near Africa, the Guanche people were also preserving their dead. The Guanches had crossed over to the islands from Morocco around 3000 BC. They used a similar method of embalming.

After removing the internal organs, they dried each body in the sun. Then, using soil, stone, vegetable matter or fat solids, they carefully prepared each body. Some were even stuffed with sand. Then each body was wrapped in animal skins. The more important the person, the more skins they were wrapped in. Kings were wrapped in as many as 15 skins. Once wrapped, the mummies were placed in caves. Stone walls were put up around the mummies to keep them safe.

burial caves

QUESTION

Why do you think people in the 1500s thought that ground-up mummies would cure stomach aches?

At one time there were hundreds of mummies in the caves around the islands. However, because of tomb raiders, only a handful of mummies now remain. Like the Egyptian mummies, most of the Guanche mummies were removed, ground up and used to make "Mummy". This was a stomach-ache remedy popular with medieval doctors in the 1500s.

HOW GUANCHE MUMMIES WERE MADE

Internal organs were removed.

Body was dried in the sun.

Body was embalmed with soil, stones, vegetable matter or fat.

Mummy was placed in a cave and surrounded by a stone wall.

Body was wrapped in animal skins.

Body was sometimes stuffed with sand.

VISUAL CHALLENGE
What other ways could you show this information?

17

Natural Mummies

Predict

What information do you think you might find out about?

Not all mummies are made by people. Some are made by nature.

One of the easiest ways to become a mummy is to fall into a peat bog. Peat bogs are deep and cold. Their water is stagnant and the top layer of peat seals off oxygen, allowing a body to mummify slowly.

Hundreds of mummies have been found in the peat bogs of northwest Europe. One of the best-preserved mummies was found in 1950 in a bog in Denmark. Named Tollund man, he was 2000 years old. He was so well preserved that stubble could still be seen on his chin and upper lip.

The oldest bog mummy on display is a woman found in the Gunhild bog in Denmark. She was originally thought to be the mummy of a Danish queen. However, tests done on the mummy in 1977 showed that she lived 1500 years before the queen, making her about 2450 years old.

Tollund man

Gunhild bog mummy

CLARIFY

peat bog
stagnant

Deserts are also good places to make mummies. The hot, dry air helps dry the body before it can decompose. Many desert tribes buried their dead in the sand or salt to mummify them naturally.

In the 1980s, 3000-year-old mummies were found in large salt pits in a Chinese desert. The mummies were of Caucasian or European origin, rather than Chinese. It is thought that they were members of an ancient civilisation that lived at the crossroads between China and Europe.

Chinese desert mummies

QUESTION GENERATE
What question might you ask about this information?

Nature has also made ice mummies. In the mid-1800s, the British Franklin Expedition set off to the Arctic with two ships and 129 men. They were never seen alive again. Their ships became stuck in the Arctic ice. The starving survivors had set off overland in a hopeless search for food and help.

In 1976, the grave of John Torrington was found on Beechey Island in Canada. He was one of the first of the Franklin crew to die. His body, buried in the ice, was exhumed in 1984 for scientific testing. Even though he had died around 130 years earlier, he was so perfectly preserved, he looked as if he was still alive, just unconscious. Scientists determined that lead poisoning from cans of food on the ship had probably contributed to his death.

Torrington's grave site

the mummy of John Torrington

uncoverin the Icema

CLARIFY

exhumed

In 1991, high in the mountains dividing Austria from Italy, two hikers stumbled across a man's body frozen in the glacier. The man, later named the Iceman, had been entombed in the ice for more than 5000 years.

The scientists who examined the body found an arrowhead imbedded in the back of the left shoulder. Some scientists believe the Iceman could have been killed in a war or as a sacrifice to gods.

By studying the contents of the Iceman's stomach, scientists were able to establish that he had eaten about eight hours before he died. His meal was a simple one of flat bread made of einkorn wheat with plants and meat.

a scientist's reconstruction of the Iceman

Iceman's tools

QUESTION
What can scientists learn about a society through mummies?

THE IMPORTANCE OF MUMMIES

treasures from Tut's tomb on museum display

Predict
In what ways do you think mummies could be important?

Protecting Mummies

For years, tomb raiders, collectors and tourists ransacked the mummies' tombs. They stole everything of value and destroyed much of what was left.
In the early 1800s, tens of thousands of cat mummies were dug up and shipped to England to be used as fertiliser.

Finally, in the 1920s, the Egyptian Government started to limit the number of artefacts that could leave the country. Today, everything excavated in Egypt is the property of the Egyptian Government.

INFERENCE
What can you infer from the following text?

In the early 1800s, tens of thousands of cat mummies were dug up and shipped to England to be used as fertiliser.

a tomb in the Valley of the Golden Mummies

This mummy is being treated with great care in the Valley of the Golden Mummies.

Archaeological digs are now carefully watched. Everything is done slowly and cautiously. Archaeologists often use soft brushes instead of drills to remove years of built-up sand and debris. Then each artefact is tagged and photographed. The artefacts from King Tut's tomb are now on display in the Egyptian Museum in Cairo, the capital city of Egypt. But mummies discovered these days are usually left, with their artefacts, in their final resting places.

In 1996, 105 mummies were discovered in the Valley of the Golden Mummies in Egypt. The find caused such an international stir and brought so many visitors to the site that archaeologists could no longer work. So they transferred a few mummies, including two young children and their father, to a nearby museum for public viewing.

QUESTION GENERATE

What questions do you have about how scientists' attitudes towards mummies have changed?

Learning from Mummies

Mummies can teach scientists a lot about the lives of people from long ago. Using tests such as body scans, carbon dating and DNA testing, scientists can now study mummies without unwrapping them. Body scans or X-rays show what amulets are buried with the body. They can also show any broken bones. For years it was believed that King Tut died from a blow to the head, but recent X-rays have found that there was a bad break in his leg. Some scientists believe that an infection from this break may have killed Tut.

DNA tests on a mummy, and carbon dating of the objects found with them, can also tell scientists when the mummy died, making it easier to work out who they were. The types of flowers buried with them show the time of year they died. And some mummies' stomach contents can show scientists how they lived and what they ate.

a CAT scan (3-D X-ray) of Tutankhamun

QUESTION

Why do you think it is important that mummies are now studied without being unwrapped?

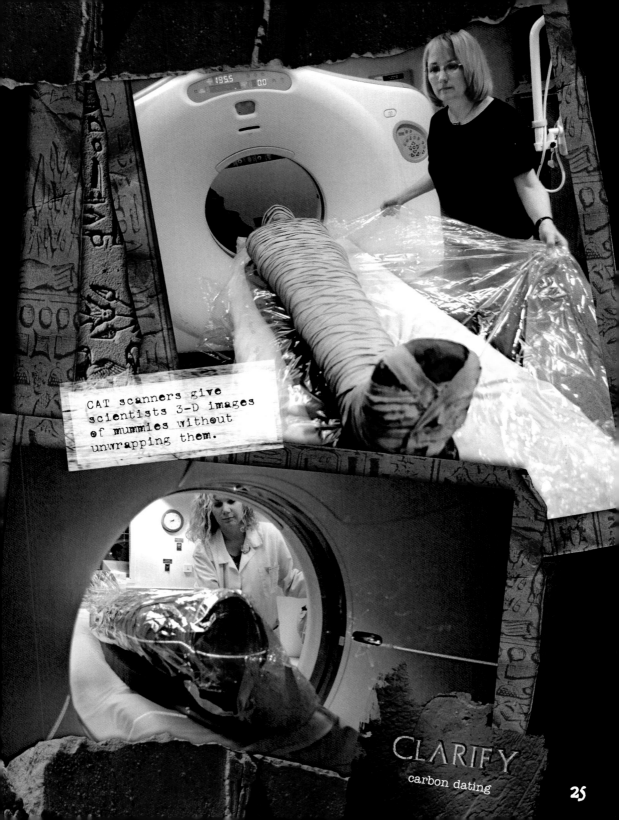

CAT scanners give scientists 3-D images of mummies without unwrapping them.

CLARIFY

carbon dating

THE MUMMY'S CURSE

The Egyptians were very superstitious. Many of the tombs of the pharaohs are said to have curses written on or around them, warning against entering. Just a few months after entering King Tut's tomb, Lord Carnarvon died suddenly. Doctors said it was blood poisoning from an infected mosquito bite on his cheek, but the European newspapers said it was the curse of the mummy. They even reported that Carnarvon's dog in England let out a howl and died at the same moment as its master.

No connection between the death of Carnarvon, who was in poor health, and any curse has been established. But it makes for an intriguing story and helps to fuel people's fascination with mummies.

INDEX

Lord Carnarvon

VISUAL RESPONSE
SEQUENCE DIAGRAM:
HOW CAT MUMMIES WERE MADE

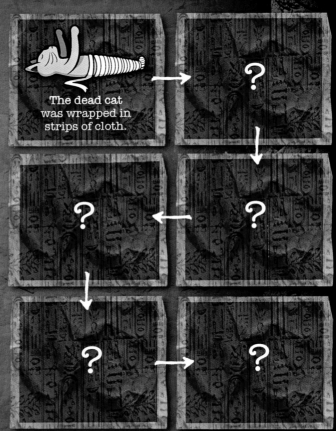

The dead cat was wrapped in strips of cloth.

Making connections – what connections can you make to the information presented in **Mummies All Wrapped Up**?

being fascinated by something different or unusual

doing a job well

having a belief

TEXT TO SELF

having a ritual

keeping treasures

finding answers

Text to Text

Talk about other informational texts you may have read that have similar features. Compare the texts.

Text to World

Talk about situations in the world that might connect to elements in the text.

PLANNING AN INFORMATIONAL REPORT

1 Organise the information

Select a topic

Mummies

What I know:

- Mummies are preserved bodies.
- Some mummies have been preserved by people and some have been preserved naturally.
- Mummies reveal a lot about cultures from long ago.

What I will research:

- Why people made mummies.
- How different types of mummies were made.
- What mummies tell us about past cultures.

2 Locate the information you will need

library

Internet

experts

3 Process the information

Skim-read.

Sort your ideas into groups.

Make some headings.

4 Plan the report

Write a general
introduction.

5 Decide on a
logical order for
your information

What will come first,
next ... last?

6 Write up your
information

7 Design some
visuals to include
in your report

You can use graphs,
diagrams, labels,
charts, tables, cross-
sections...

WRITING AN INFORMATIONAL REPORT

Have you . . .

- recorded important information?

- written in a formal style that is concise and accurate?

- avoided unnecessary descriptive details, metaphors or similes?

- used scientific or technical terms?

- written a logical sequence of facts?

- avoided author bias or opinion?

Don't forget to revisit your writing. Do you need to change, add or delete anything to improve your report?